THE MAJESTY OF NATCHEZ
POSTCARD BOOK

By Steven Brooke

D1475233

PELICAN PUBLISHING COMPANY
GRETNA 2005

First printing, March 1998
Second printing, March 2005

The word "Pelican" and the depiction of a pelican are
trademarks of Pelican Publishing Company, Inc., and are
registered in the U.S. Patent and Trademark Office.

ISBN: 9781565543409

Printed in China

Published by Pelican Publishing Company, Inc.
1000 Burmaster Street, Gretna, Louisiana 70053

Stanton Hall, Natchez

PHOTO BY STEVEN BROOKE © PELICAN PUBLISHING CO., INC.

To:

The House on Ellicott's Hill, Natchez

To:

Magnolia Hall, Natchez

To:

Child's bedroom, Rosalie, Natchez

To:

The Parsonage, Natchez

To:

Texada, Natchez

PHOTO BY STEVEN BROOKE © PELICAN PUBLISHING CO., INC.

To:

Green Leaves, Natchez

To:

Shields Town House, Natchez

To:

The Burn, Natchez

To:

Place
Postage
Stamp
Here

Double parlor, Routhland, Natchez

To:

Auburn, Natchez

PHOTO BY STEVEN BROOKE © PELICAN PUBLISHING CO., INC.

To:

Place
Postage
Stamp
Here

Dunleith, Natchez

To:

Arlington, Natchez

PHOTO BY STEVEN BROOKE © PELICAN PUBLISHING CO., INC.

To:

Linden, Natchez

To:

Monmouth, Natchez

To:

Montaigne, Natchez

To:

Place
Postage
Stamp
Here

D'Evereux, Natchez

To:

Place
Postage
Stamp
Here

Varina Howell married Jefferson Davis in 1845 in this front parlor at The Briars, Natchez

To:

This piano at Richmond in Natchez was used to accompany Jenny Lind during a performance in 1851

To:

Longwood, Natchez

PHOTO BY STEVEN BROOKE © PELICAN PUBLISHING CO., INC.

To:

Elms Court, Natchez

PHOTO BY STEVEN BROOKE © PELICAN PUBLISHING CO., INC.

To:

Gloucester, Natchez

PHOTO BY STEVEN BROOKE © PELICAN PUBLISHING CO., INC.

To:

Place
Postage
Stamp
Here

Glenburnie, Natchez

PHOTO BY STEVEN BROOKE © PELICAN PUBLISHING CO., INC.

To:

Fair Oaks, Natchez

To:

Elgin, Natchez

To:

Place
Postage
Stamp
Here

Lansdowne, Natchez

To: